Let's Look At
Series
Edited by Robert Owen

LET'S LOOK AT

Prehistoric Animals

LET'S LOOK AT

Prehistoric
Animals

Alan R. Warwick

Illustrated by Norma Ost

ALBERT WHITMAN & Company

Chicago

First published in Great Britain in 1966 by
Frederick Muller Limited, Fleet Street, London E.C. 4
Copyright © 1966 by Alan R. Warwick
First published in the United States by
Albert Whitman & Company
L.C. Catalog Card Number 67-26522

Also in this series:

Let's Look at

CASTLES *Alan R. Warwick*

COSTUME *Edmund J. Cooper*

PUPPETS *A. R. Philpott*

Foreword

This is a subject which takes us right back to the very beginnings of life on our planet. With every discovery it has become richer and more breathtaking. This story has been told for all time in stone—a picture history of the wonderful, often weird and nightmarish creatures which inhabited this earth a hundred million years and more ago. For, fortunately, their forms have been preserved in the rock-formations—fossilised shapes that speak with exact detail of long-extinct animals, amphibian, reptile, and bird, that populated both land and sea.

They passed into final oblivion seventy million years ago, yet their appearance and behaviour and way of life is as clear as if human eyes had beheld them.

There are still great gaps to be filled, but each year the picture of the living past grows clearer and more vivid.

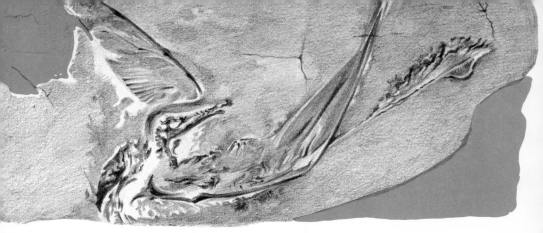

Fossilised great flying reptile—rhamphorhynchus

Once upon a time. . . .

The story starts like a fairytale, but it is not a fairytale. Far from it. It is the story of those strange and often grotesque creatures that populated the earth hundreds of millions of years ago. Some lumbered with massive tread. Others flew with umbrella-like wings of stretched membrane. Others, again, swam and hunted in the ancient seas. Some of these creatures were as huge as houses; others were as small as mice.

It is a story that takes us back to the very beginnings of life on our planet.

But how do we really know that those long-ago strange creatures ever really existed?

That is part of the remarkable story. Those long-dead ancient animals have left accurate traces of themselves in the form of their own fossilised remains. They have left exact impressions on solid rock, which tell us what they were like and something of their way of life.

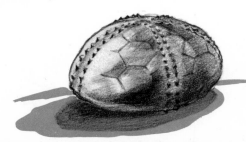

Fossilised sea urchin

The rocks in which fossils are to be found are the kind that are termed sedimentary rocks. They were formed from the tight packing together of small bits of sediment, such as clay, or chalk, or lime. The fossils found embedded in those rocks are of animals that sank into the soft ooze and became covered up by it. Later, under tremendous pressures the sediment turned into hard rock, such as sandstone, limestone, shale, or slate.

The fossil itself was created by the tissues of the creature being gradually replaced by mineral matter infiltrating and taking on the exact shape and form. Thus the original body of the creature—whether animal or vegetable—is replaced by a stone replica.

Siberian mammoth—found frozen and intact

PLEISTOCENE PERIOD

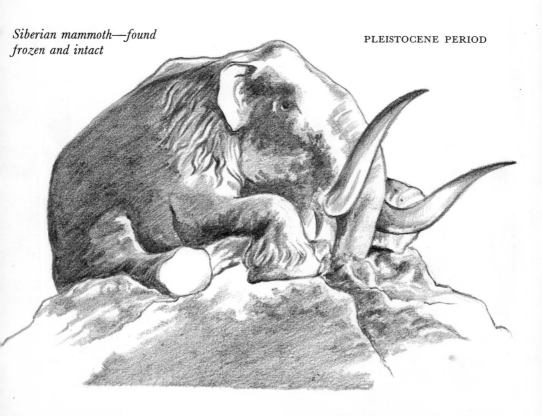

The story of prehistoric life has been slowly and carefully unravelled by men and women whose work it has been to study the rock formations in the earth and the fossils contained in them. These men and women are called geologists.

Quite tremendous skeletons have been found, and their exact age determined. Some ancient skeletons, notably the dinosaurs, are more than 80 feet long, the bone segments turned to stone.

Things huge and things small have all contributed to the picture of the past. The exact appearance and delicate outline of the wing-feathers of ancient birds have been found clearly imprinted on the surface of what is now hard rock. The outstretched wing, bones and membrane, of prehistoric flying reptiles have likewise left their detailed imprint. These impressions show us the shape and texture of those animals as they were in life. The very footprints of tremendous reptiles that stalked the earth have been recorded, the soft clay over which they walked now hardened to stone.

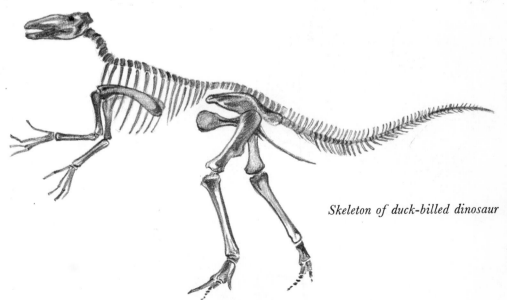

Skeleton of duck-billed dinosaur

Many years ago I watched a dalmatian dog walk over a patch of freshly smoothed cement, leaving the marks of his pads on the surface. That dog must now be long dead, but his footmarks remain sharp and clear to this day. I asked a man who was a judge of dogs if he could decide what kind of dog made those footmarks.

'A dalmatian,' he replied, and described in detail the dog I had seen all those years before.

Bit by bit the story of the past has been pieced together into a clear picture, like arranging the pieces of a jigsaw in their right order. There are gaps in the overall picture, nevertheless the pattern has grown steadily in detail, showing the progress of life on this planet from its first beginnings.

Well, how did it all begin?

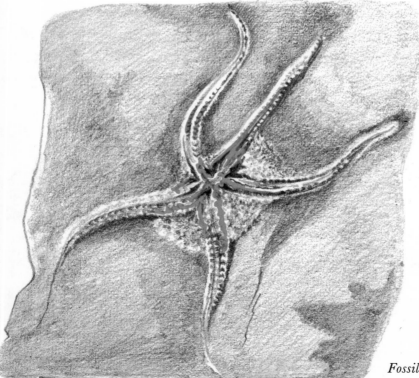

Fossil of star-fish

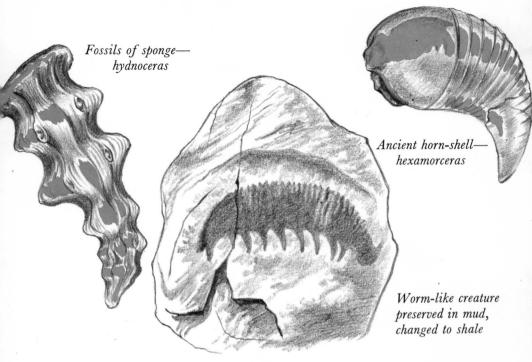

Fossils of sponge—
hydnoceras

Ancient horn-shell—
hexamorceras

Worm-like creature
preserved in mud,
changed to shale

Scientists tell us that about 6,000 million years ago our planet was a spinning globe of gases revolving round the sun.

Myriads of years rolled by and the whirling gases became liquefied under vast pressure. At last our planet's surface cooled into a solid crust. It is estimated that the crust formed about 4,500 million years ago. It consisted of granite-like rock which had once been molten and was still glowing with heat.

As can be imagined, one will never find fossils in that kind of rock, which is known as igneous rock, meaning that it was produced by fire.

Footprint of
thinopus antiquus

Surrounding our planet at that time would be a steamy atmosphere containing little or no free oxygen, and heavy with water vapour. Oxygen, such as we breathe, was only to be added much later. It is thought that certain single-cell creatures, early plants and, later, the great forests which covered much of the land surface, consumed carbon dioxide and gave off oxygen.

EARLY CAMBRIAN PERIOD

Trilobite and leaf fossils

Millions of years went by after the first cooling of the earth's crust. The water vapour in the atmosphere began to be squeezed out as the temperature dropped, so that it fell to the ground in great drops. In other words, it began to rain!

Such rain, once it started, must have been tremendous and continuous, rather like the story of Noah's flood. As it splashed and swished down it would help further to cool the earth's surface. Rivers and wide shallow seas were formed.

They would hardly have been like the rivers and seas we know today. There would be no sign of growing things on the rocky land—no grass or vegetation of any kind to make the river banks green. Nor would there be sandy beaches to fringe the shallow seas. Sand was only to come later when water and weather had ground rocks to powder.

The actual seas themselves were of fresh water. Salt had yet to be dissolved from the rocks.

The great rain period

Period	Date	Life and Creatures
ARCHEOZOIC	Period beginning approx. 2,000 million years ago.	No creatures. Great volcanic activity.
PRE-CAMBRIAN ERA	Era beginning approx. 1,125 million years ago.	Seaweeds and primitive forms of sea life.
CAMBRIAN	Period beginning approx. 500 million years ago.	Small marine creatures continued.
ORDOVICIAN	Period beginning approx. 440 million years ago.	Sea urchins, sea snails, corals, sponges.
SILURIAN	Period beginning approx. 380 million years ago.	Earliest known plants. Fish-like creature with *backbone* appeared.
DEVONIAN	Period beginning approx. 300 million years ago.	Sea full of fish. Ferns and horsetails appeared.
CARBONIFEROUS	Period beginning approx. 250 million years ago.	Large insects including dragonflies.
PERMIAN	Period beginning approx. 205 million years ago.	Some plants and creatures became extinct. First fossils of lizards discovered from this period.

Plan of Prehistoric Periods

Period	Date	Life and Creatures
TRIASSIC	Period beginning approx. 170 million years ago.	Main plants—ferns, conifers, cycads. Insects. Dinosaurs appeared.
JURASSIC	Period beginning approx. 135 million years ago.	Many dinosaurs. Flying reptiles, archaeopteryx. First true mammals.
CRETACEOUS	Period beginning approx. 95 million years ago.	Giant dinosaurs.
PALEOCENE AND EOCENE	Periods beginning approx. between 80 and 50 million years ago.	Dinosaurs became extinct. Mammals most important land creature. Plants began to appear as we know them today.
OLIGOCENE	Period beginning approx. 42 million years ago.	Ancestors of pig, camel, rhinoceros and sabre-toothed tiger.
MIOCENE	Period beginning approx. 25 million years ago.	Rapid growth of animal life—including large elephants, armadillos, giant sloth—many insects.
PLIOCENE	Period beginning approx. 8 million years ago.	Man-like apes appeared.
PLEISTOCENE	Period beginning approx. 500,000 years ago.	Primitive man. Mammoths.

Plan of Prehistoric Periods

To our eyes it would have been a grim-looking world.
Nevertheless, gradually the earth's surface was being made
ready to receive the life which it yet lacked. With millions
more years to pass, with water and weather wearing down
mountains and hard rocks, with internal earth pressures
forcing up new mountain ranges and new land levels, with
volcanoes spouting lava, and a warm, humid climate covering
all the world, the most important—and certainly the most
mysterious—event in the whole history of our planet took
place. More than 600 million years ago life made its first
appearance on this earth.

It was life in its simplest form, neither animal nor vegetable,
perhaps rather like a virus, which has some of the qualities of
living things and some of the qualities of non-living things.
From that first beginning was to evolve all the varied life in
the world.

General view of country in Pre-Cambrian times

Those first faintest traces of earliest life have been found in rocks which are so old as to be among the very earliest of stratified rocks. They are what are known as pre-Cambrian, and are more than 600 million years old.

How this first birth of life happened nobody knows. Some scientists think that if certain chemical and physical changes take place under the right conditions a form of life will inevitably take place. They believe that if all the processes through which the earth went from its original state of gases were to be exactly repeated, life would once more appear.

Be that as it may, what is certain is that something happened that turned what had been previously lifeless matter into something that had the power to feed on surrounding matter and so grow and multiply. Every so often a little speck of living thing would divide itself and turn into two specks. Two specks would become four, and so on.

Much later what are called single-cell creatures began to appear in the warm shallow seas. That era is called the Palaeozoic, or Old Life. It is an era which lasted for 375 million years.

Those single-cell creatures were themselves neither animal nor vegetable, but they were the forebears of all animal and vegetable life in the world. They were minute, jelly-like blobs in the sea, and increased their numbers by the simple method of dividing themselves into two.

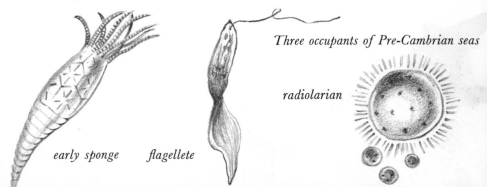

Three occupants of Pre-Cambrian seas

radiolarian

early sponge *flagellete*

Ammonite

By ways that still can only be guessed at, those single-cell creatures later on became primitive seaweeds and such animals as jellyfish and star-fish and a form of sea-worm.

It is thought that in the process of evolution groups of single-cell creatures united together forming themselves into one organism, rather like sponges or coral. In these organisations the cells would adapt themselves to certain functions— some to find food, others to eat it, others to digest it, while others would be occupied in producing new creatures after their own pattern.

Other forms of sea-life came into existence, such as sea-scorpions, sea-snails, and an early form of crab. They were all animals without backbones.

Fossilised jellyfish

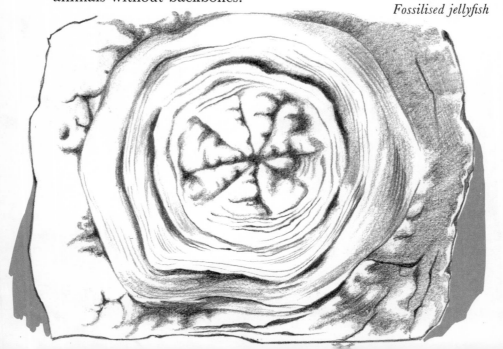

Seaweeds were adapting themselves to other circumstances. From the seashore they were slowly able to move up over the land and take root there, ceasing to be seaweeds and becoming land plants of a primitive fern type.

In like manner sea-scorpions and sea-centipedes and other creatures of the water were adapting themselves. The shore-line where the tides ebbed and flowed enabled them to leave the water and to crawl and hop about on the wet shore. The first land animals were wingless, such as early scorpions and mites. Then, later, came great dragonflies with a wing span of 20 inches or more. There was also a variety of cockroach, and various types of fly, as well as spiders and snails.

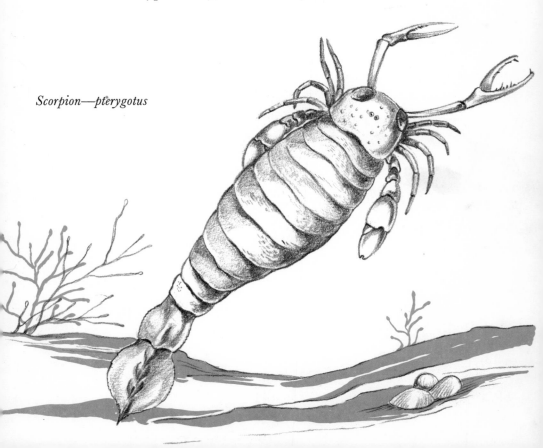

Scorpion—pterygotus

As this first invasion of the land took place, so insect life and vegetation increased. Mighty forests grew prolifically in the humid, warm atmosphere that prevailed all over the world. They consisted of great ferns and giant mosses, which eventually were to form the vast coal seams and oil reserves which lie under the earth's surface.

Strangely different those forests must have been from the ones we know, with only the hum of insects to disturb the silence, and the great dragonflies in place of birds.

While all this was going on, below the surface of the waters Nature was preparing another important evolutionary development. Up to that time all animals had been invertebrates, which is to say that they were animals without backbones. The time had now come for animals with backbones to appear.

Just consider yourself for a moment. You have a backbone. You have two legs and two arms. You have two eyes and a mouth. So has your cat and your dog. Horses, cows and sheep are of the same pattern. Tigers, lions, elephants—all mammals have the same general formation.

Early Silurian sea creatures

This particular pattern is called the tetrapod or four-legged pattern, and it is shared by all creatures with backbones. The highest forms of life are those that possess a backbone. Such a body is more mobile and possesses a far more highly developed nervous system. Furthermore, the backbone ends in a skull which has space provided for a brain.

DEVONIAN PERIOD
Forest of great ferns and giant mosses

With the evolution of the backbone an entirely new type of animal came into existence. It possessed greater agility, greater speed and, above all, greater intelligence.

The first creature with a backbone was a fish. It was a very primitive fish, without jaws or teeth. It could only suck, such as a lamprey does, or a leech. Nevertheless, it was the forerunner of more advanced fish armed with jaws and teeth. With the evolution of the backbone the Age of Fishes had begun, and it lasted for 100 million years.

As fishes evolved and adapted themselves to the varying conditions that affected their lives, there chanced to be a species which had a sort of air-sac behind the throat. This acted as a primitive lung, and air gulped in would supply oxygen to the blood. So, unlike its companions, the fish with an air pocket was able to pop its head out of water and gulp air.

This was to prove a life-saver under changing conditions.

It is probable that if everything had remained as the fishes first found them, there might never have been any four-footed animals on land. The fishes would have had no reason to leave their natural surroundings as long as food was obtainable and there was adequate water in which to swim.

Primitive fish—anglaspis

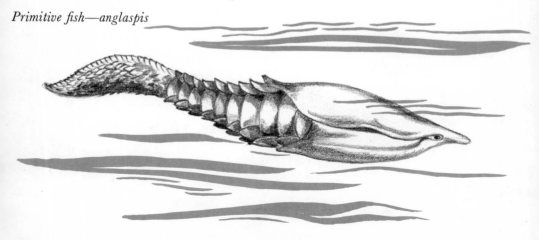

But just as life had not remained static, and was continually pressing on to something new, so the world outside was also changing. About half-way through the Palaeozoic era, between 350 and 400 million years ago, in what is called the Devonian period, there were long intervals of many years when no rain fell.

Rivers and swamps and marshes began to dry up, and for the most part the fishes caught in those drying-up pools died. But the lung-equipped fish were more fortunate. They could gulp air to get their oxygen that way. Also, their fins were strongly developed in a very specialised way, so that they were able to use them like primitive legs and crawl out of their drying-up water holes. It was necessity that drove them, and they dragged themselves off in search of other pools with a better water supply.

Furthermore, they were flesh-eating creatures armed with strong jaws and teeth, and they would be able to find food to devour on the way. Dying fish left high and dry on the banks of the diminishing water holes would certainly provide those fierce fish with all the food they needed.

Those lobe-fin fish, as they are called due to the special muscular arrangement of their pairs of fins which they were able to use as legs, became the forerunners of an entirely new breed of animals—the amphibians.

Primitive fish—pterespis

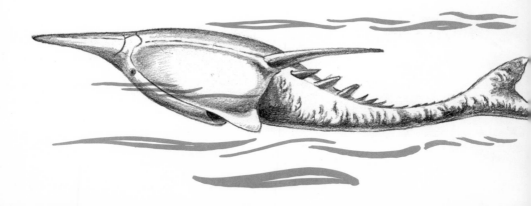

Frogs and newts and toads that you find in ponds and wet grass and under stones are, of course, present-day amphibians. They can live quite comfortably out of water so long as they remain cool and damp. Like fish, they are what are termed cold-blooded animals. Their blood temperature is the same as that of their surroundings. In cold weather they grow sluggish. When it is too cold or too hot they die. With warm-blooded animals, such as human beings and cats and dogs, the blood temperature normally remains level.

Though amphibians can live on land, they must always return to water to lay their eggs. The frog-spawn you see floating in a pond has a jelly-like outer coating, which protects and holds the egg itself. Those eggs would quickly dry out if they were laid on land, and the embryo would die.

Amphibians—ichthyostegids

There is another reason why amphibians must lay their eggs in water. When the young hatch out they are like fish, and breathe by means of gills. It is only later that the amphibian lung and other characteristics develop and the gills disappear. From then on the amphibian can only breathe air.

But to return to the lobe-fin fish and the first amphibians. As the two pairs of specialised fins turned into legs the membranes which joined the small bones at the ends of the fins gradually disappeared and toes and claws were formed.

The first amphibians to invade the land, which until then had only been populated by insects and other invertebrates, were quite small. Some of them were not more than a few inches in length from head to tail. They were not unlike present-day newts, but in the course of ages there developed monster amphibians 15 feet or more in length.

These new animals occupied the marshes and the forests surrounding them. Because of the shape of their legs, which were awkwardly placed at the sides of their heavy bodies, with knees and elbows sticking outwards instead of forwards and backwards, they could only crawl over the ground. Nevertheless, they were quite powerful, with strong jaws and teeth, and in their day they were the lords of the forests.

Lobe-fin fish

As millions of years passed many varieties of amphibians were evolved, and they persisted for 100 million years as the dominant form of life on land. They varied in extremes of sizes from a few inches to 15-foot giants. One species, not more than 5 inches from head to tail, became the ancestor of the newt. Another, a mere 3 inches in length, was the forebear of frogs and toads. Fossils of amphibians with a long body and tail, but with a characteristic frog's head have been found in Triassic period strata of 200 million years ago. Other fossils, found in Kilkenny, Ireland, are of amphibians which had dispensed with legs and took on the appearance of snakes, some being 3 feet long.

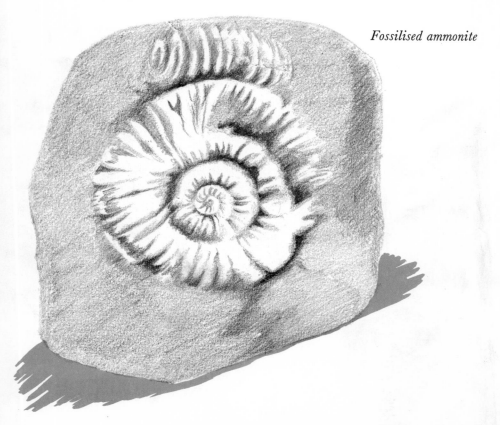

Fossilised ammonite

Amphibian—orphiderpeton

In some ways it was an advantage for an amphibian to be a small size. On land great body weight was a handicap for legs that were more suited for swimming than walking. In the water was quite another matter, for there the animal was relieved of its own weight. It floated. An amphibian is a compromise between a land animal and a fish. It has, of course, the advantages of two worlds, but the difficulty is that it does not swim as well as a fish, nor does it walk as well as a land animal.

It is hardly surprising that the giant amphibians became extinct. They continued into the Triassic period but they had grown huge and fat, and their legs were feeble. They had almost abandoned living on land, and wallowed in the lakes.

These last amphibian giants were the eryops and the mastodonsaurs. The former were up to 7 feet in length, while the latter, which came later, were 10 feet or more.

Their heads were enormous and out of proportion. They had degenerated, as though the ancient amphibian stock were wearing out after so long an existence. But it was the harsh heat of the Triassic sun that finally shrivelled them into extinction, leaving only the smaller, more agile varieties to carry on the species.

Eryops

That, however, is but one aspect of the story of the amphibians. One must see what happened to another branch of that great order of animals in the progress of evolution.

There lived in the Permian period a certain animal which measured about $2\frac{1}{2}$ feet from head to tail. It was an amphibian in many of its aspects, but it possessed some other features.

Thus, instead of the eyes being set on top of the skull, an amphibian characteristic, this animal's were at each side of its head. Furthermore, in place of the sprawling amphibian legs, the limbs were better arranged for walking on land. Knees tended to be more forward, elbows farther back. Instead of crawling, this animal could waddle, and make better speed.

Nature had, so to speak, produced a more efficient and up-to-date model!

Mesosaur

The fossil remains of this new animal were found near the town of Seymour in Texas, U.S.A., and consequently it has been given the name seymouria as its identification label.

As an animal it was a great improvement on the previous amphibian pattern, and its trump card was something quite remarkable. Amphibians, as we know, must always return to water to lay their eggs. The penalty of this is they can never move very far from water. The seymouria was startlingly different. It got over the problem by laying a new sort of egg!

This novel egg, instead of being coated with jelly, was contained in a shell that was full of liquid. In that liquid was the embryo, attached to a yolk from which it drew its nourishment. This was a most convenient arrangement, for it meant that from now onwards eggs could be laid on dry land, while the little creature inside it, until it was ready to emerge from the shell, remained snug in its own private pond!

When it did emerge it came in contact with the outside air as a fully formed land animal in miniature. It had passed through its gill stage while still in the egg.

This, as you can see, was a great evolutionary step forward. For the first time animals with backbones were freed from having to return to water as part of their life cycle. Consequently their range of living space, and opportunities for finding food, were greatly extended.

The seymouria has been hailed as the missing link between the amphibians and reptiles. A reptile means literally a crawling animal! All reptiles can live on land or in water, and have a backbone, lungs for breathing and a skin covered with scales. Seymouria might be so considered, though it does not tell us *how* the change was made from producing amphibian eggs to dry land eggs. That is still a mystery. Nevertheless, the seymouria marks the dawn of the Age of Reptiles. Itself, it was half amphibian, half reptile, but fossil records show that there were true reptiles living at the same time as the seymouria. It can only be presumed, therefore, that true reptiles and the seymouria had a common ancestor. That ancestor is the missing link.

Seymouria

The first known reptile was one that has been named the cotylosaur. It was a primitive form of reptile that became extinct about 240 million years ago, but from it evolved the immensely wide variety of reptiles that were to be the lords of the earth for nearly 150 million years.

It is perhaps convenient at this point to divide the descendants of the cotylosaur into five groups, each of which can, to some extent, be dealt with separately. It simplifies somewhat the general description of what is a complicated subject. So to begin with, let us take a line of descent from ancient reptiles that has experienced the least change, namely the turtles.

From what the fossil records show, it is evident that turtles arrived at their familiar shape about 220 million years ago.

Their typical shells, which are intimately connected with the animal's skeleton, are of bone, overlaid with a covering of horn. The shell is in two halves which are joined together. The top half is termed the carapace, and the lower half the plastron.

As a means of protection from enemies the shell has been most successful. In all the millions of years since the turtle appeared on the scene there seems to have been only one major improvement. The earlier forms of the turtle were not able to retract their heads and limbs into the protection of the shell. That came later.

From the vantage-point of carapace and plastron, in which speed had been surrendered to all-round defence, the family of turtles have prospered and lived, unaffected by the many and sometimes fantastic changes that have distinguished their reptilian cousins—evolutionary changes which, while producing such extravagances as the largest land animals the world has ever seen, also often led to total extinction.

Turtle—archelon

Today there are more than two hundred varieties of tortoise and turtle. They are truly prehistoric animals that have lived almost unchanged on into the twentieth century. They were there when the first flying reptiles glided and wheeled and flapped on leather wings; they witnessed the fantastic age of the dinosaurs; they saw great reptiles return to the waters as marine monsters; and they continued to live their way of life when all those creatures passed into oblivion.

The second great line of reptiles began to develop a marked change in its appearance, and no doubt a corresponding change in its cold-blooded nature. That was 180 million years ago, at the beginning of the Jurassic period. The remarkable thing that happened was that it began to look less like a reptile and more like a dog!

That creature is called a cynodont. Some were only a foot long, while others grew to 7 feet or more in length. In build, they were rather long in the body and short in the legs, with a long tail. They ate meat, and they developed teeth rather like a dog's teeth. Their reptile jaws changed to dog jaws.

Mammal-like reptile—cynodont

Eohippus, 'dawn-horse'

Some of the later mammal-like reptiles could curl up like a dog, which was a very un-reptilian thing to do. It is believed that it was from them that the warm-blooded animals were evolved. If that is so—and it seems most likely—it means that all mammals: dogs, cats, horses, human beings, were descended from that dog-like reptile.

There was another important development in that mammal-like reptile. It possessed a specialised roof to the mouth that is termed a secondary palate.

The secondary palate is a characteristic of all mammals, but is absent in reptiles. It forms the roof to the mouth, leaving a separate air passage between the nostrils and the back of the throat.

By this arrangement mammals are able to chew their food and breathe at the same time, which is essential for warm-blooded animals to do. Reptiles, lacking that secondary palate, are forced to gulp their food and air spasmodically when feeding.

The behaviour of an animal is governed by whether it is cold-blooded or warm-blooded. The one possesses quite a different make-up from the other. A reptile's mind is fundamentally different from a mammal's, and is of a lower order.

Amphibians and reptiles because they are cold-blooded have no constant body temperature. They become as cold or as warm as their surroundings. Out of water their own physical efforts raise their body temperature very quickly.

When that happens the creature is brought to a halt so as to cool down. Reptiles, for that reason, cannot make long continuous journeys. Usually they move slowly and deliberately, and can only be very active in fits and starts. Watch a lizard. See how it runs for a few feet and then remains quite still.

Warm-blooded animals, on the other hand, are able to maintain continuous activity for long periods. They also possess greater mental alertness. Those superior qualities may indeed have helped towards the final extinction of the great reptiles of Cretaceous times. It was that period that saw the end of the dinosaurs; and the close of the Age of Reptiles was followed by the Age of Mammals. Until then warm-blooded animals had been in a very minor position.

First known crocodile—protosuchus

The third line of descent from the cotylosaur evolved in a direction entirely different from those previously described, for they gradually abandoned life on land and returned to the water. They became highly efficient marine animals.

Their legs became modified into flippers that were fin-like, and the tapering reptile tail became fish-like in shape. A vertical fin-like crest appeared along the backbone, and the entire animal became as streamlined as a fish. Those marine reptiles are called ichthyosaurs, and fossil remains show that they grew to a length of 30 feet or more. They must have been magnificent swimmers, and very formidable in their quest for food, which would be fish.

Though they came to look very like fish, that does not mean they went into an evolutionary reverse and moved backwards through the amphibian stage to become fishes once more. That was not possible. Evolution is a one-way process, though it is open to a multitude of adaptations. Those marine animals remained air-breathing reptiles, while taking on an external form somewhat like a present-day dolphin, but with long-pointed jaws armed with teeth.

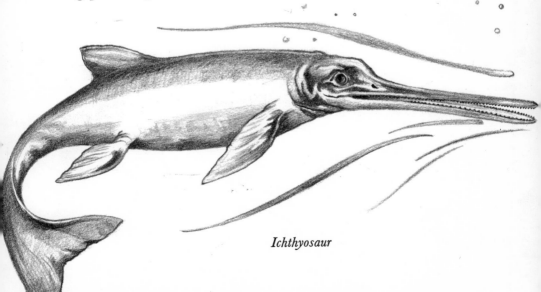

Ichthyosaur

In their evolution to marine creatures, ichthyosaurs became what is termed ovoviviparous. Instead of laying eggs, later to be hatched, the young were hatched out within the mother's body and were born ready for swimming.

The babies were probably born near the surface of the sea for they were air-breathing, and they would have drowned if they had not been brought to the surface in quick time.

As a species, the ichthyosaurs became extinct about 80 million years ago. Why that should have happened to them no one really knows, for ichthyosaurs were well adapted to marine life, just as much, seemingly, as the present-day dolphin or porpoise which they so resembled.

Like the whales, they are all instances of land animals returning to a watery environment, the chief difference being that the ichthyosaurs were cold-blooded reptiles while the later creatures are warm-blooded mammals.

In the fourth line of descent from the first primitive reptile, fossil remains once again reveal a prehistoric animal that forsook land life to return to a watery one. That creature is named the plesiosaur. It, too, achieved well-developed flippers to take the place of legs, and with these it rowed itself through the water.

It was an enormous animal, and must have looked rather like the drawings one sees of the alleged Loch Ness monster. It had a small head at the end of a very long neck, which was 20 feet long, or thereabouts. The neck was about half the total length of the animal; beyond the rounded body the tail tapered to a point.

Plesiosaur

The plesiosaur's swimming speed was probably not great, nothing like as fast as the ichthyosaur's. It would cruise with its head and the top of its back just out of the water—again, very like drawings of the Loch Ness monster—but it would dart its long flexible neck swiftly in any direction when hunting, and seize its prey with its sharp teeth.

It probably spent much of its time in shallow water near the shore, and it laid its eggs in the sand after the manner of the turtles.

There was a cousin to the plesiosaur which had a large head and a short neck. That was the placodus, a 5-foot long marine creature which spent its time dredging the bottom of the shallow water in search of shellfish. Those it crunched up with its powerful grinding teeth.

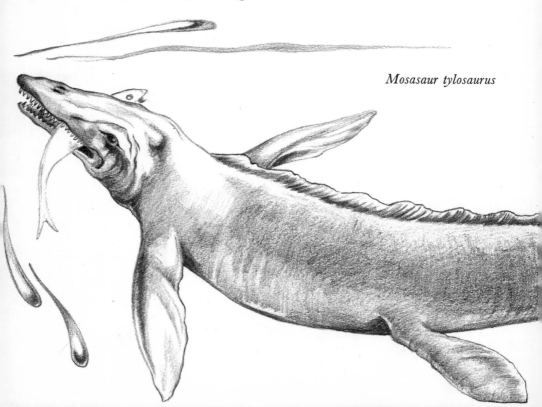

Mosasaur tylosaurus

The sea at that time abounded in marine reptiles of all shapes and sizes, and it would seem that they made a very good living. Another animal, the geosaur, was a sea-going crocodile with flippers and a fishtail. It had crocodile-like jaws and teeth, and was 30 feet long. An equally ferocious animal was a marine lizard, called the mosasaur tylosaurus, about 50 feet in length. It had a flexible tail with a fin running down its length, and it propelled itself through the water with its flippers. The jaws were somewhat beak-like in shape and furnished with sharp teeth, and it was altogether a terrifying animal.

Among all those sea-going animals of strange and fearful shape were the familiar turtle, some so huge that the shell alone was 12 feet long.

With the exception of the turtle, all these exotic marine creatures became extinct near the end of the Cretaceous period, which had lasted for 65 million years and marked the end of the Mesozoic (Middle Life) Era. The turtles, however, continued as marine creatures for millions of years more, when, in the Caenozoic (New Life) Era some of them returned to a life on land. Their flippers became modified back to legs, and they turned into tortoises.

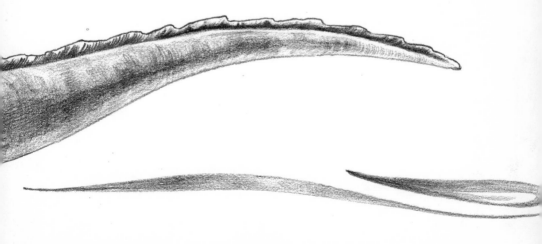

We now come to the fifth great group of reptiles descended from the original cotylosaurs. This is by far the largest group, and over the millions of years it produced the widest range of creatures. Today there are five living descendants of that group. They are crocodiles, birds, lizards, snakes, and a rare New Zealand reptile called sphenodon. At one time there were vast numbers of them, but men slaughtered so many of them that they were near to extinction and are now under rigid government protection.

That crocodiles and birds should be descended from the same stock and be, as it were, cousins, may sound very surprising, but it is true. There are visible signs of the bird-reptile relationship. Thus, some of the great reptiles of the past had bird-like feet after the manner of ostriches, and they possessed beaks similar to birds. Tortoises, as you have probably noticed, have rather bird-like beaks, while the scaly legs and claws of birds are definitely reptilian, and their skeletons in various ways reveal their reptile ancestry.

Unfortunately, less is known about the origin of birds than of other creatures. There are relatively few fossil remains of ancient birds. It is known, though, that 150 million years ago there were birds with toothed beaks and long reptilian tails on which feathers grew. Also there were claws on the leading edge of the feathered wings which were the remains of earlier fingers.

Rare New Zealand living reptile—sphenodon

Two flightless birds from different periods

Moa (Pleistocene)

Diatryma (Eocene)

The reptile origin of birds has been arrived at largely by comparing creatures. The lack of bird fossils is due to the fact that birds then, as now, mostly lived on land. When they die and fall to the ground their remains are usually eaten by scavengers, or are destroyed and scattered by wind and weather.

With sea birds, on the other hand, of those that die on the water their skeletons became more often buried in the mud and silt. Consequently they were more likely to end up as fossils. It is mostly from such fossils as those that the history and reptile origin of birds is deduced.

Birds were not the only creatures of the air 150 million years ago, for at that period, the Jurassic, there were a large number of flying reptiles with wings of skin stretched from the body to the arms and digits. Flying reptiles and birds were of two quite separate evolutions, with the advantage going to the birds. Reptile wings were more vulnerable to injury than birds' wings. Damaged feathers would not necessarily cripple a bird's flight, and they could be replaced by new growth, but a torn wing membrane would be certain to prove fatal to the reptile.

Both birds and flying reptiles originated from the thecodont ancestor, which was also the ancestor to the dinosaurs. Those remarkable flying reptiles, which took on varied forms, among them the later celebrated pterodactyl, were light in construction. The bones, though hard and compact, were hollow, and air from the lungs would circulate through them.

Pterosaurs is the name given to all the race of flying reptiles, which came into existence in the Triassic period about 170 million years ago, which was 20 million years before the first known trace of birds. Apart from the winged insects, which made their appearance in the Carboniferous period 280 million years ago, flying reptiles were the first animals to take to the air.

There is in this respect, however, one fundamental difference between insects and all other flying creatures. Insects possess what are called true wings. That is to say, such wings were designed by Nature specifically for flying. Those Carboniferous insects hummed and flew through the prehistoric forests, almost playing the part of birds. Some of the dragonflies had a wing span of more than 20 inches.

For over 100 million years flying insects held undisputed sway in the air, until the pterosaurs were evolved with their membrane wings which produced an airfoil surface between the outstretched arms and the sides of the body and short legs.

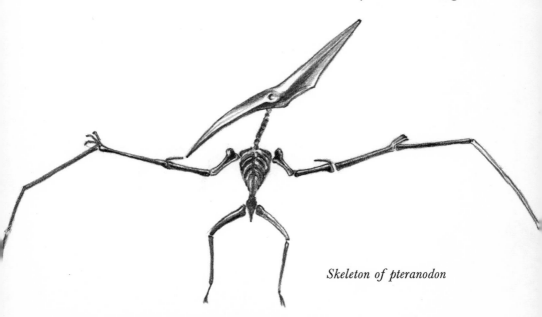

Skeleton of pteranodon

Tremendous extension of the wing span was achieved by great elongation of the fourth or 'little' finger on each of the pterosaur's hands. The arms and the fourth fingers provided the leading edges of the membrane wings, while the remaining three fingers were free to act as claws.

At first glance a pterosaur's and a bat's wings are much the same. But only superficially. The big difference between a pterosaur's wings and those of a bat is that with the bat all the fingers are included in the actual framework of the membrane wings. The spaced ribbing of their membrane wings makes them stronger against accidents and more umbrella-like when extended.

Archaeopteryx (forerunner of bird)

Birds and pterosaurs evolved separately from a common ancestor. It is perhaps not difficult to imagine how the membrane of a pterosaur's wing evolved, just as web-foot was evolved, but the development of a bird's feathers remains a mystery to this day. That the latter was a better system of providing an airfoil cannot be doubted. The wing of skin supported by one elongated finger was undoubtedly more vulnerable to crippling damage than a feather wing.

Phororhacos (flightless carnivorous bird)

In the million years of their existence, those flying reptiles took on many shapes. There were those with long lizard tails. One variety had a rudder-like flat surface at the end of its tail used for steering itself in flight. There were other flying reptiles with hardly any tail at all. Some had long beaks almost like a heron's; others were constructed like those of a raven or a puffin. Some had teeth in their beaks; others were without teeth.

In all instances the legs were practically useless for walking, though the animals could probably climb trees by creeping up on all four sets of claws. As bats do, they may have used their rear claws by which to hang upside-down when sleeping.

These strange flying creatures varied enormously in size, but grew larger as time went on. Some were as small as a robin, while others, such as the pteranodon, had a wing span of about 28 feet. Such a wing span made the pteranodon the largest animal ever to fly.

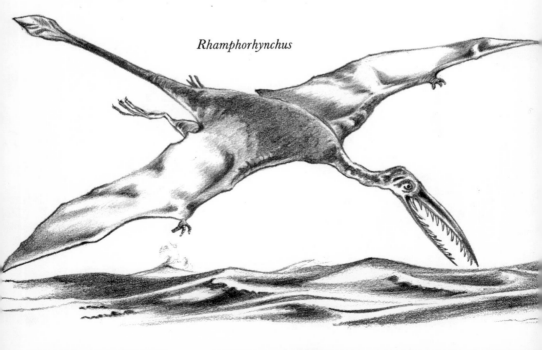

Rhamphorhynchus

As with birds, they laid eggs, and it is thought that the helpless young would be reared in a manner similar to that of birds. Pterosaurs may even have made rudimentary nests, though they probably laid their eggs on inaccessible ledges after the manner of sea birds. They would no doubt do all their hunting on the wing, swooping down from their resting places and gliding over the lakes and shallow seas much as sea birds do today, snatching their prey with their toothed beaks.

And then at last they perished, every one of them, leaving the air for the undisturbed use of their cousins the birds. They passed into extinction with their other relations, the dinosaurs.

Pteranodon

The dinosaurs in their time were quite the most impressive section of the reptile family tree. It is those great reptiles, which dominated the earth for so many millions of years, that make the pattern of prehistoric creatures so dramatic and spectacular.

They were, as we have said, closely related to the birds and flying reptiles as well as to the crocodiles, for they shared a common ancestor called the thecodont, which in its turn descended from the more primitive cotylosaur.

The thecodonts lived during the Triassic age, which places them about 100 million years later than the cotylosaurs. They were small animals, far from spectacular in appearance, the biggest not more than 3 feet in length, but they spread prolifically over the shallow waters and surrounding lands of that period.

Conditions then were hot and dry, with great desert areas, and sudden deluges of rain to fall on parched earth. There were at that time no polar ice-caps. It was the beginning of a new era of life, namely the Mesozoic, in which many new creatures and groups of creatures made their appearance.

The thecodonts that lived on land tended to become bipedal or two-legged. They walked and ran on their hind legs, balancing themselves with their long tails, with the result that the front limbs became small and frail, while the hind legs grew strong and muscular. Most of them developed a protective armour of one sort or another.

Edaphosaurus and ornitholestes (in background)

Another branch of the thecodonts, known as the phyto-saurs, took to the water, and in leading an aquatic existence became curiously crocodile-like, though in fact they were not the forebears of the true crocodile, which evolved quite separately. True crocodiles, which were bigger and stronger and even better adapted to their river-bank surroundings, supplanted the phytosaurs and saw them fade into extinction.

Most of the land reptiles of the Jurassic and Cretaceous periods of the Mesozoic Era are loosely termed dinosaurs. Under that popular generalisation they form sharply defined groups. Some were colossal creatures that walked on four legs, and were browsing, vegetarian animals, as was shown by their teeth, other dinosaurs walked on two legs.

Of the latter some were vegetarian, while the others were flesh-eaters, and were provided with sabre-sharp cutting teeth.

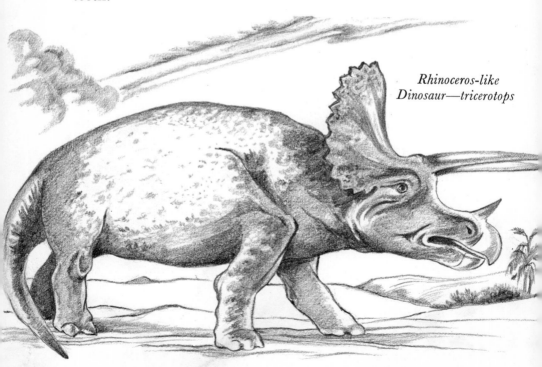

*Rhinoceros-like
Dinosaur—tricerotops*

Those two great groups of dinosaurs are called respectively the saurischia and the ornithischia. Both came from the same ancestor, but evolved on different lines. Thus, the saurischia had pelvic bones on the usual reptile plan, though some were two-legged and carnivorous, while others of the group were huge, slow-moving, and walked on four legs, and were vegetarian.

The ornithischia were different from the saurischia in the formation of the pelvis, as well as in other ways. They, too, had two- and four-legged varieties. They were without armour, and the entire group was vegetarian.

Corythosaurus

It is a law of life that vegetarian animals are the prey of hunting animals. They become their source of food. The zebra and the gazelle provide food for lions. In the same way the vegetarian dinosaurs were the prey of the carnivorous ones. Fossilised skeletons of browsing dinosaurs have been found with the sabre-like tooth marks on them made by the teeth of their carnivorous attackers. No question how such unfortunates died!

One of the most tremendous animals the world has ever known was the brontosaurus. It weighed as much as 40 tons, and was nearly 70 feet from head to tail. It fed on vegetation, and because of its tremendous weight, as much as for self-defence against carnivorous attackers, it lived most of its time in the comparative safety of the waters of the lakes.

It was a slow-thinking creature with a minute brain in relation to its vast size. Believe it or not, its brain was no bigger than an egg! Its natural enemy was a carnivorous dinosaur, the allosaurus.

Brontosaurus

The meat-eating allosaurus, 35 feet long, was armed with savage teeth and terrible cutting jaws. It was quicker-moving than the brontosaurus, and had a quicker brain. It ran on two legs, the feet of which consisted of four claws rather like those of a bird. The short arms were equipped with three-fingered talons. As a creature, it was utterly savage, and any brontosaurus that fell into its clutches was very soon a dead dinosaur.

Dinosaurs dominated the world for 100 million years, and in that long time evolution produced many successive varieties. Fifty million years after the brontosaurus came the truly terrible tyrannosaurus, which was like a vast allosaurus. When walking on its two legs, its head was 20 feet from the ground. The teeth in its jaws were 6 inches long, and its total body length was 50 feet.

Allosaurus

That terrible reptile hunter lived in the Cretaceous period, and was therefore among the last of that grisly race. Its scaly feet were equipped with three taloned toes in front and a fourth shorter one at the back. They were bird feet. The minute arms, so short that it seems likely that they could not reach the animal's mouth, had but two clawed fingers to each hand. No doubt those tiny arms and hands were useful for some specialised purpose, but for what we do not know. Nevertheless the tyrannosaurus was a formidable and terrifying creature.

One of the most enormous animals that ever lived in the Age of Dinosaurs was the brachiosaurus. It had a length of 82 feet and a height of 42 feet. It weighed 50 tons and lived on vegetation. Unlike the usual tendency among dinosaurs, this animal's front legs were longer than the back. All four legs terminated in massive beast feet with five broad toes.

The neck was extremely long and terminated in a very small head which contained a minute brain. Its means of defence, it would seem, was to submerge itself in the waters of the lake with only its eyes and nostrils above the water.

To aid it in this its eyes were set high on top of its head with the nostrils raised on a hump just above the eyes. When submerged up to the eyes its presence would go undetected by its enemies.

Within the last hundred years much has been learned about prehistoric animals. At the Crystal Palace in London can be seen some wonderful reconstructions of prehistoric animals. These were constructed by Mr. Waterhouse Hawkins in 1853 who built them up from the latest scientific information of the time, such as was given by the then celebrated Professor Owen.

However, much more has been learned since then, consequently, there are inaccuracies to be found in those wonderful models.

Tyrannosaurus

On New Year's Eve, 1853 Mr. Hawkins gave a dinner party inside the lower half of the cast of the iguanodon, with Professor Owen seated at the head. That gives you some idea of the huge size of the monster, for the belly of the model held about a dozen gentlemen seated at dinner.

The finished model of the iguanodon is to be seen to this day by the Crystal Palace lake, and very impressive it is. But there are two major inaccuracies. Thus, the front legs and the back legs are the same length, whereas it is now known that the front legs of the iguanodon were much shorter than the back legs. The animal was bipedal, and the front legs were used as arms.

Waterhouse Hawkins' iguanodon presents the dinosaur with a short horn at the end of its nose, something like a rhinoceros tusk. And it looks very impressive and realistic there. But guess where it ought to be! It is now known that the conclusion Professor Owen came to as to the position of that horn was wrong, and that it was, in fact the animal's thumb! It was a much later fossil discovery in Belgium that discovered that important truth.

The horny thumb was that vegetarian creature's main weapon of defence against its carnivorous enemies, notably the megalosaurus. If an attack were made by that ferocious monster the iguanodon could rip up its enemy's flanks with those two terrible spikes.

These two animals both existed in Cretaceous times, and such battles between them—for they were much of a size—must have been earth-shaking.

Other leaf-eating dinosaurs had other means of defence against enemies. Many of them developed massive armour of bone or horn. The polacanthus, a short-legged creature, was protected by a dramatic array of massive spines in two rows down its back and tail. With its tail it could make savage defensive cuts which would inflict terrible damage on any incautious attacker.

A similar creature, called the palaeoscincus, also had short legs, and was heavily armour-plated. It was ringed all round with spikes extending down its strong tail which ended in a tremendous club. This strange-looking creature, which only wanted to be left alone to eat its vegetarian meals, could defend itself in no uncertain manner by delivering a smashing blow with the club end. Any limb in the path of that swinging club would be dreadfully shattered.

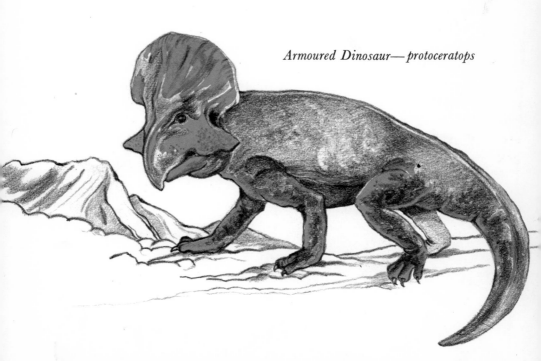

Armoured Dinosaur—protoceratops

The name of the group of armoured reptiles, of which the polacanthus and the palaeoscincus were two, was the ankylosaurus. The dinosaur of that name was quite enormous, horned and armoured, being as big as two elephants. It was from the ankylosaurus that the whole range of armoured dinosaurs of this description descended.

Some of those creatures took on quite incredible shapes as a means of defence against enemies. There was the stegosaurus, a monster with a tapering lizard head and tremendous plates of bone arranged like a double crest along its back. In earlier times the animal had been bipedal, but as the plates grew more and more massive during progressive evolution the animal was finally compelled to return to the all-fours position to carry the load.

Nevertheless, it was a formidable looking creature 30 feet long, with four tremendous spikes growing out of its strong-looking tail. It would seem that one flip of its tail would be certain death to any animal it might strike, but as to whether it could use its tail in that manner is doubtful. The peculiar interlocking construction of the vertebrae suggests that such a method of defence might not be possible. If that is so, then it seems that those spikes were the ultimate absurdity of decoration.

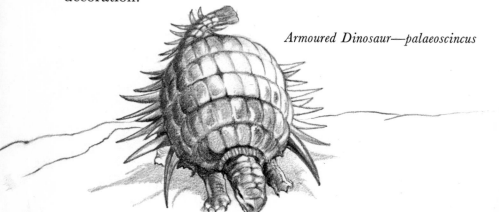

Armoured Dinosaur—palaeoscincus

Armoured Dinosaur—stegosaurus

Like so many others, the stegosaurus was not notable for its intelligence. Its brain was about as big as a peach. To make up for this, and to give the animal some control over its own body, the spinal cord, which extended from the head to the tip of the tail, was fortified with two subsidiary brains. They were sort of relays from the main brain. These relays controlled the legs and the tail. Both the secondary brains were larger than the main brain.

Stegosaurs spread over all parts of the world, and their fossil remains are everywhere to be found. They died out 135 million years ago during the fateful Cretaceous period.

This strange armour-plating of vegetarian dinosaurs went on for 100 million years, the protective plating becoming increasingly cumbersome and exaggerated, until finally extinction overcame them as it did all the rest of the strange reptile giants.

It was just as if they had lived too long and had become too massive to find sufficient food to sustain their giant frames. There were other changes at work as well. Land masses altered and the sea overwhelmed many areas. The climate was altering, and in place of the early plants with leaves that grew all the year round, the new type of deciduous tree, which shed its leaves in the winter months was taking their place. Such a change in food supply might well represent starvation to groups of animals that were unable to adapt themselves to changing conditions.

If the vegetarians died then the carnivorous animals that lived on them would also die of starvation.

And so the story of the reptiles as the world's dominant population came to its end.

Prehistoric reptiles on land, in the sea, and in the air, had a history that extended over 200 million years, which shows that so long as it lasted they were well adapted to living, and it was only change that beat them. The history of the prehistoric animals is one of the major occurrences on this globe.

Seventy million years ago the story ends, and what is termed the Caenozoic (New Life) Era came in. Mammals moved into the living space vacated by the great reptiles, and gradually took over the populating of the world.

One million years ago an ape-like creature sat chipping a stone to get a sharp edge on it. He had developed sufficient intelligence to make himself a crude knife of flint with which to cut up his prey for food. That chipping of stone was a sign that new masters of the world were on their way in.

Prehistoric Man

INDEX Italics indicate illustrations.